HOW TO IMPROVE AT PLAYING
PIANO

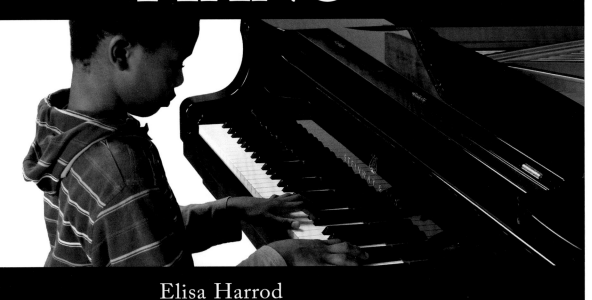

Elisa Harrod

Crabtree Publishing Company
www.crabtreebooks.com

Author: Elisa Harrod
Editor: Dan Green
Consultant editor: Stephen Coombs
Proofreader: Marion Dent
Editorial director: Kathy Middleton
Designer: Rob Green
Indexer: Michael Dent
Prepress technician: Margaret Amy Salter
Production coordinator: Margaret Amy Salter
Production controller: Ed Green
Production manager: Suzy Kelly

Produced by dangEditions
All music copyright © TickTock Entertainment Ltd 2010

Photo credits:
All photographs by Andy Crawford except:
Redferns/Getty Images: page 47
iStock: pages 4 (top), 6 (bottom), 9 (top)
CSU Archives/Everett Collection/Rex Features: page 46
Shutterstock: pages 4 (bottom right), 4 (bottom left), 8 (red notes),
9 (red notes), 18 (middle)

The publisher would like to thank Junior Guildhall for their help in the
production of this book. In particular: Derek Rodgers, Alison Mears, and
James Wilson. They would also like to thank Stephen Coombs for his
advice and help in the production of this book.
Guildhall students: Millie Ashton, Christopher Brewster, Johan Clubb,
Zara Hudson-Kozdoj, Jessica Liu, Marie Luc, Yosi Philip-McKenzie,
Chantal Osindero, Didier Osindero, Rebekah Rayner, Marianne Schonle

Library and Archives Canada Cataloguing in Publication

Harrod, Elisa
    How to improve at playing piano / Elisa Harrod.

(How to improve at--)
Includes index.
ISBN 978-0-7787-3579-3 (bound).--ISBN 978-0-7787-3601-1 (pbk.)

    1. Piano--Instruction and study--Juvenile.
I. Title. II. Series: How to improve at--

MT745.H323 2010   j786.2'193   C2009-907186-X

Library of Congress Cataloging-in-Publication Data

Harrod, Elisa.
  How to improve at playing piano / Elisa Harrod.
      p. cm. -- (How to improve at--)
  Includes index.
  ISBN 978-0-7787-3601-1 (pbk. : alk. paper) -- ISBN 978-0-7787-3579-3
(reinforced library binding : alk. paper)
  1. Piano--Instruction and study--Juvenile. I. Title.
  MT745.H37 2010
  786.2'193--dc22

                                    2009049737

Crabtree Publishing Company
www.crabtreebooks.com   1-800-387-7650

Published in Canada
Crabtree Publishing
616 Welland Ave.
St. Catharines, Ontario
L2M 5V6

Published in the United States
Crabtree Publishing
PMB 59051
350 Fifth Avenue, 59th Floor
New York, New York 10118

Printed in the U.S.A./012010/BG20091216

CONTENTS

STEINWAY & SONS

INTRODUCTION

Welcome to the amazing world of making music. Music is something that is played, listened to, and enjoyed all over the planet whether it's dance music, traditional, classical, or good old rock and roll. Being able to play and create music is a skill that will bring you and others a lot of pleasure. You're ready and willing, so let's take steps to improve your playing!

BUILDING SKILLS

This book will help you build your piano skills, beginning with the basics, then move on to more advanced techniques. On the way you will find new techniques and skills, plus exercises to help you develop and progress.

HOW TO USE THIS BOOK

Nothing could be simpler! Use the contents page opposite to make this book work for you. You can work through page-by-page, or leap ahead to work on a particular skill or play a piece. Step-by-step guides show you proper technique; the custom-written piano pieces then help you practice them.

TOP TIP BOXES

Watch for these helpful boxes, which give you extra information on technique.

TECHNICAL TERMS BOXES

All technical terms and musical signs and symbols are explained in these boxes.

THE PIANO

Before you start playing, it is important to know something about your instrument and how it is set up. There are a lot of parts to a piano. Although you don't need to know what every one of them does in order to play, it is still really useful to know their names and understand what they do.

EARLY KEYBOARD INSTRUMENTS

Before the piano was invented, harpsichords were the most popular keyboard instruments. The strings inside a harpsichord are plucked, making it sound completely different than a piano. Then, in 1700, an instrument maker named Bartolomeo Cristofori came up with a way for the strings to be hit with a hammer instead of being plucked. This new sound was smoother than a harpsichord. The piano was invented.

UNDER THE LID

Underneath the lid of any piano are two sets of strings—a set of short strings for making high treble notes, and a set of long strings for making low bass notes.

Harpsichords were favorite instruments in royal courts and everyday parlor rooms until the 1800s.

Experiment for yourself—take an elastic band, stretch it tight, and pluck it. If you stretch the band tighter or make it shorter, you get a higher sound. Depending on the length and tightness of the elastic band, you can create different notes.

string   hammer

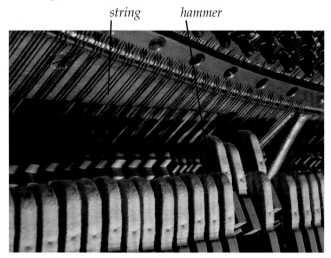

Inside a piano, each note is made with a set of two or three strings, each with its own hammer.

With the lid raised, it's easy to spot the long (bass) and short (treble) strings inside a grand piano.

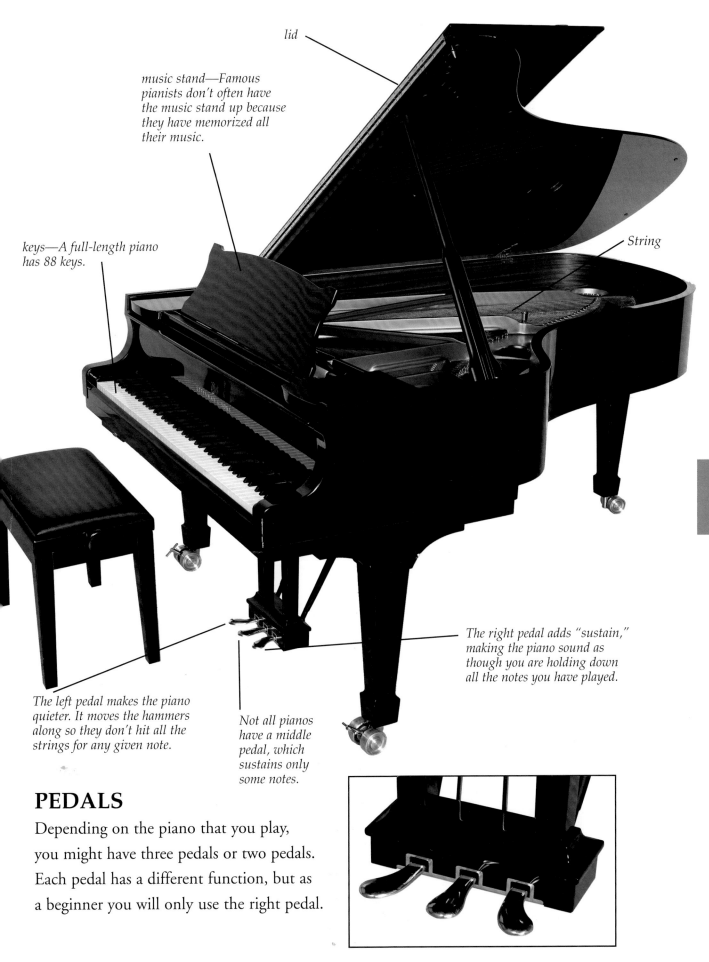

lid

music stand—Famous pianists don't often have the music stand up because they have memorized all their music.

keys—A full-length piano has 88 keys.

String

The right pedal adds "sustain," making the piano sound as though you are holding down all the notes you have played.

The left pedal makes the piano quieter. It moves the hammers along so they don't hit all the strings for any given note.

Not all pianos have a middle pedal, which sustains only some notes.

PEDALS

Depending on the piano that you play, you might have three pedals or two pedals. Each pedal has a different function, but as a beginner you will only use the right pedal.

GETTING STARTED

Practice and mental attitude lets us improve any hobby or skill. The most important thing to remember is that practice should be fun! It is all about enjoying music. Sometimes it is challenging, but you should always feel rewarded by your progress. Here are some top tips to get you going.

Planning counts

Before you start practicing, plan out what you are going to do:
- *Which exercises or scales are you going to warm up with?*
- *What sections of your pieces are you going to work on?*
- *What piece are you going to reward yourself with playing at the end of your practice? This should be something you can already play and really enjoy.*

Five times rule

This rule really works! If you can play a tricky part five times in a row, then you have got it nailed. If you make a mistake though, you go back to zero.

Regular as clockwork

Try to practice 10–15 minutes every day.

Slow down

Do everything slowly until you get the hang of it. If it all gets too much, then take a break and try again later.

Mental attitude

It's really important to want to improve. Practicing requires discipline, but the rewards are worth it. You will develop a skill you will have for the rest of your life.

PREPARING TO PLAY

Since you will be sitting down to play, it's important that you sit properly at the piano. Getting your posture right will also help you be comfortable and able to relax. Next run through a few warm-up exercises before you start. Then you will be ready to go.

SITTING UP STRAIGHT

A correct posture keeps you alert and improves your playing. Make sure that your stool does not move or swivel and is not too high or too low. You should be able to reach the keys comfortably without leaning forward.

WARMING UP

If you were going to run a race, you would warm up first to be at your best. Warm up your fingers before you play the piano and you'll get a lot more out of your time.

Warm-up routine

- *Pick different warm-up exercises for each practice.*
- *Pick a couple of scales to run through.*
- *Once you can play the warm-ups, challenge yourself to play them faster.*
- *Try them out **legato** and **staccato** (see pages 16–19).*

Technical terms

*Signs and symbols on a music score tell you the **dynamics** of a piece of music—how loud or quiet to play.*

p 'piano' – *quiet*	*ff* fortissimo – *very loud*
mp mezzo-piano – *quite quiet*	
mf mezzo-forte – *quite loud*	crescendo – *get louder*
f forte – *loud*	
	diminuendo – *get quieter*

RHYTHM

If you take your pulse, you can feel your heart beating regularly. This steady pulse is like a beat in music. Different types of notes are held for different numbers of beats to create different rhythms.

GET INTO THE GROOVE

STEP 1

Tap along to a favorite piece of music. Once you're in time, you've got the beat of the music.

Note lengths

𝅝   *whole note = 4 beats*

𝅗𝅥   *half note = 2 beats*

♩   *quarter note = 1 beat*

♪   *eighth note = ½ beat*

𝅘𝅥𝅯   *sixteenth note = ¼ beat*

𝅘𝅥𝅮𝅘𝅥𝅮   *two quavers = ½ + ½ = 1 beat*

Eighth notes

Don't be tempted to play eighth notes as fast as you can. Usually, eighth notes are grouped in twos or fours, so practice clapping two claps to every beat—that's an eighth note.

STEP 2

Try clapping this rhythm:

STEP 3

If all music was written as one long line of notes, like the one above, it would get really confusing. Lines divide up music into "bars" of equal numbers of beats. Clap this rhythm:

STEP 4

Bar lines should be invisible to the listener—don't pause when you get to them. Now clap out this rhythm. Can you recognize what children's nursery rhyme it comes from?

BASIC SKILLS

TIME SIGNATURES

Not all pieces have four beats in a bar. At the beginning of every piece of music the **time signature** tells you how many and what type of beats are in each bar.

The top number shows how many beats are in the bar.

The bottom number shows what type of beat it is. A "4" means it is a quarter note, and an "8" means it is an eighth note.

See if you can clap the following exercises:

Dotted notes

When you see a dot after a note, it means hold this note for half its value again. So a half note with a dot would be 2 beats + 1 beat (half a half note) = 3 beats.

♩.   3 beats

♩.   1½ beats (or 3 quavers)

Rests

These are the symbols for rests in music:

Rest for whole bar or 4 beats   ▬

Rest for 2 beats   ▬

Rest for 1 beat   𝄽

Rest for a half beat (½ beat)   𝄾

9

RHYTHM & TIME SIGNATURES

TREBLE NOTATION

In music, notes are written on five lines called a "staff." Treble notation shows the high notes above middle C on the piano keyboard, which are usually played with your right hand. Dive in and learn how to find these notes on the keyboard.

NOTES ON THE TREBLE STAFF

Ledger lines are extra lines used when the notes go beyond the five lines of the staff.

staff

C D E F G A B C D E F G A B C

This is the treble clef sign. It usually relates to notes above middle C that are played with your right hand.

NOTES ON THE PIANO KEYBOARD

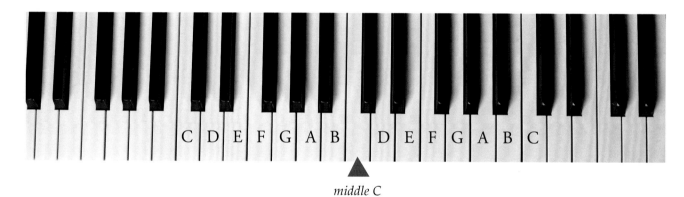

C D E F G A B D E F G A B C

middle C

BASIC HAND POSITION

STEP 1

Each digit on your right hand is given a number. Starting at number one for the thumb, the numbers work outward to five. Now place your hand on the piano keyboard.

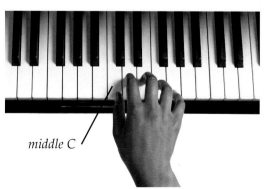

middle C

STEP 2

For the basic hand position, place your right-hand thumb on middle C and each finger on the notes above it. Middle C is the closest C to the middle of the piano.

10

STEP 3

Always make sure your hand is in a good rounded position. An excellent way to check this is to cup your hand on top of your knee, then lift it onto the keys—keep that rounded shape and keep your wrist flat.

STEP 4

Test your knowledge of notes on the piano keyboard by finding and playing the treble clef notes shown below as quickly as possible.

C D E F G A B C D E F G A B C

STEP 5

Play through these treble clef exercises. It might be a good idea to clap through the rhythms first.

Ready reference

*Come back to these pages as you work through the book.
They will help you work out any notes you are unsure of.*

EXERCISE 11.1

EXERCISE 11.2

EXERCISE 11.3

EXERCISE 11.4

TREBLE NOTATION

BASS NOTATION

Now on to the bass clef. Bass notation relates to the low notes below middle C on the piano keyboard. These are usually played with your left hand.

NOTES ON THE BASS STAFF

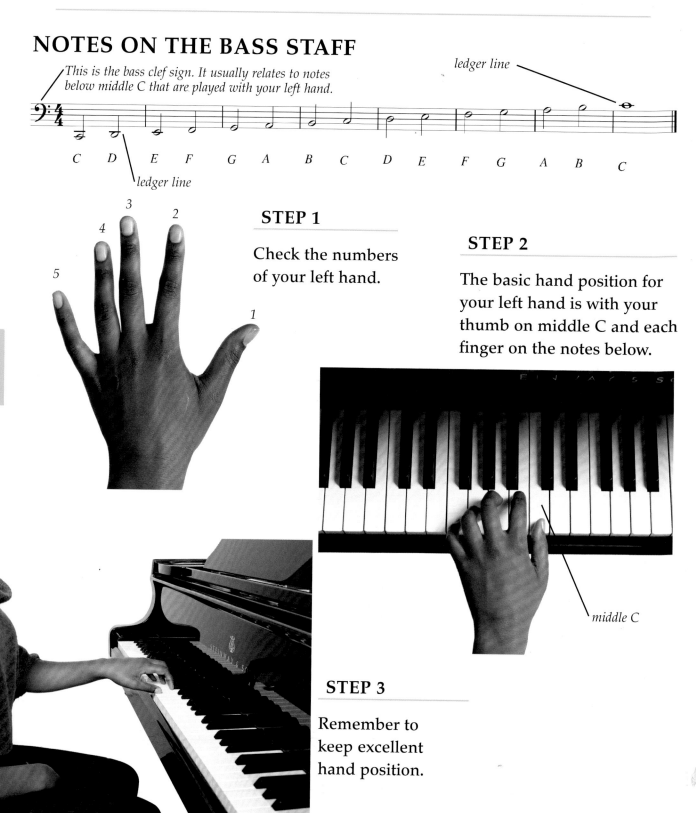

This is the bass clef sign. It usually relates to notes below middle C that are played with your left hand.

ledger line

ledger line

C D E F G A B C D E F G A B C

STEP 1

Check the numbers of your left hand.

STEP 2

The basic hand position for your left hand is with your thumb on middle C and each finger on the notes below.

middle C

STEP 3

Remember to keep excellent hand position.

STEP 4

Try finding and playing these bass clef notes as quickly as you can.

STEP 5

Now try these bass clef exercises. Clap through the rhythms first to get
an idea of how they go.

EXERCISE 13.1

EXERCISE 13.2

EXERCISE 13.3

EXERCISE 13.4

HANDS TOGETHER

Putting both hands together is the first really big step you will take when learning to play the piano. Almost every piece of music you can name has separate parts for your right and left hands. Mastering this technique will unlock a whole new world. Remember, practice makes perfect!

BEGINNING SLOWLY

Here are two exercises with basic hand positions (thumbs on middle C) to practice hands together:

STEP 1

Look at the time signature. How many beats are in a bar?

STEP 2

Slowly practice each hand separately, using the Five Times Rule (*see* page 6).

Place thumbs on middle C

STEP 3

Put both hands together. Start very slowly at first, putting the parts together bar by bar.

ONE MORE EXERCISE

SHIFTING HAND POSITIONS

As you get better at playing, you will be asked to move your hand into a different position and onto a new set of notes, all within the same piece. Don't panic—just figure out before you begin where your hands should start, and where and when they should change position.

Master the technique

When moving up or down a scale, you can shift your hand position easily to reach the notes by slipping your thumb underneath your hand onto the next note (RH going up/LH going down), or by moving your 3rd finger over your thumb (RH going down/LH going up).

When shifting hand position, lift your hand completely off the keyboard. Make the movement strong.

Be sure to give yourself enough room when passing your thumb under your hand.

THUMB UNDER

These exercises will help you practice changing hand positions:

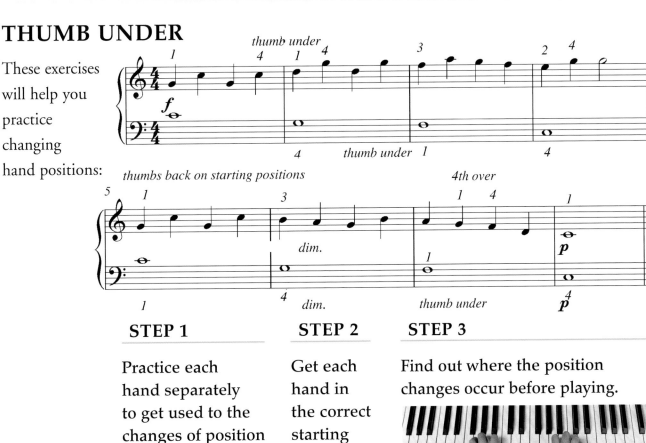

STEP 1	STEP 2	STEP 3
Practice each hand separately to get used to the changes of position before putting your hands together.	Get each hand in the correct starting positions.	Find out where the position changes occur before playing.

PLAYING LEGATO

Now that you understand basic rhythm, treble and bass notes, and hands together, you are ready to add style. Legato is a smooth and polished playing style that will have you sounding like a professional.

SMOOTH AND STYLISH LEGATO

There are lots of different ways to play a piece of music—loudly or softly, animated or laid back, slurred or choppy. Legato means to play smoothly, with all the notes running together sweetly, making sure there are no overlapping of notes or gaps between them.

Smoothly does it

To get the best results, try to keep a good hand position, and let your fingers move smoothly without getting tense.

Try playing these exercises as smoothly as possible. Imagine each finger stepping directly from one note to the next.

Slurs

A slur is two notes held together by a curved line. It means the notes contained inside the curve should be played without a separation.

EXERCISE 16.1

EXERCISE 16.2

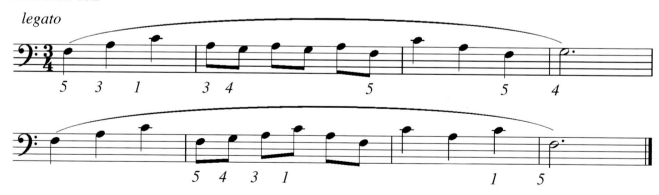

D.C. al CODA

CODA ⊕

D.C. al Coda *means first go back to the beginning until you get to the* CODA *sign, which is a circle with a cross. Then go to the* CODA *bars to finish the piece.*

16

STARLIGHT:

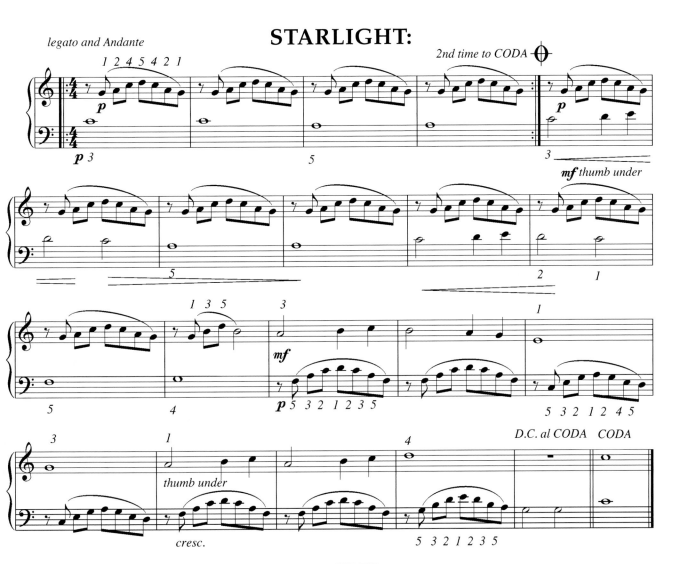

legato and Andante

2nd time to CODA

mf thumb under

D.C. al CODA   CODA

thumb under

cresc.

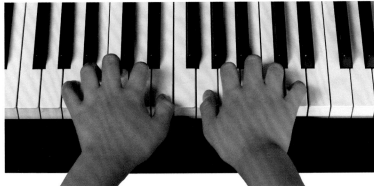

STEP 1

Work out which position your hands should start in before you play.

STEP 2

Practice each hand separately first, making sure the notes are correct.

STEP 3

Check your hand movements in the piece. Here are the hands at bar 15.

STEP 4

Now bring both hands together and practice very slowly.

PLAYING LEGATO

PLAYING STACCATO

Staccato notes are short and separated—you should be able to hear a gap in between them. When you see a note with a dot above or below it, it means play it in a staccato style.

CHOPPY STACCATO

STEP 1

To play in a staccato style, imagine that you are bouncing a ball. Keep your wrist relaxed, and try this, with your hand in a playing position.

STEP 2

Now try playing this way with every finger of both hands.
Is one hand better than the other?

STEP 3

Now try playing these exercises in a staccato style.

Mind tricks

Think about the piano being really, really hot. The minute you touch it—ouch! Take your fingers right off!

EXERCISE 18.1

This means to continue in the same style (i.e. staccato)

EXERCISE 18.2

HAPPY HOPPING

Hand position

Remember to keep a good hand position with your wrist relaxed. Try not to move your arms up and down when your fingers play staccato notes.

STEP 1

Practice each hand separately.

STEP 2

The trick with this piece is to nail the rhythm. At the beginning, think "left, right, left, right," etc. In bar three, think "left, right, left, right, left, right, together, right."

STEP 3

In bar seven, you need to play two notes with your right hand at the same time. Practice this separately and remember to keep your wrist relaxed.

TAKING IT FURTHER

Piano pieces come with all sorts of different time signatures. You have already tackled time signatures with three and four beats to a bar, but the more time signatures you play, the more skillful you will become!

DAYDREAMING

STEP 1

Place your hands on the keyboard in this starting position for *Daydreaming*.

STEP 2

At bar 13, your hands should be in this position.

SHAPES IN MOTION

Time check

Remember that 6/8 means there are six eighth notes in a bar.

STEP 1

Prepare yourself to start this piece by placing your hands on the keyboard in this position.

STEP 2

Think about getting the notes right, then add dynamics. In bar nine, you reach this position.

TAKING IT FURTHER

FINGER STRENGTH

Keen football or basketball players need to keep in shape, and playing piano is no different. Here are exercises you can do to help your fingers gain strength, agility and flexibility, while keeping them relaxed and tension-free!

SHAPE UP!

Choose a finger and rock from that finger to another a few times. Then move on to the next finger. Try the following exercise using the little finger on your right hand:

EXERCISE 22.1

Now try starting with your 4th finger, going up to your 5th, then to your 3rd, 2nd, and 1st.

Building agility

Concentrate on playing the notes evenly. Check that your hand position is rounded and that it's your fingers doing the work.

EXERCISE 22.2

MUSICAL SIGNS

There are so many things to think about when you are playing, such as the notes, the rhythm, the time signature, and dynamics. On top of that, you can add the musical signs and expressions that tell you how to play the piece! Here are the meanings of some signs you will come across:

accents—When you see this sign above or below a note, it means emphasize the note and make it stand out.

repeat—This sign has already appeared in the pieces we have played. It means repeat or go back to.

start repeat

end repeat

D.C. al Fine—Go back to the beginning of the piece until you reach the word '*Fine*', which means "finish" or "stop"

D.C. al Fine

TEMPO INSTRUCTIONS

Instructions on a piece's **tempo**, or speed, are put at the beginning unless the pace changes in the tune. For historical reasons, most instructions are in Italian. Here are some of their meanings:

Technical terms

presto—Very fast tempo

vivace—Lively and fast tempo

allegro—Quick, lively

allegretto—Fairly quick

moderato—Medium pace

andante—Quite slow, at a walking pace

adagio—Slow tempo

largo—Even slower

rit—This is short for ritardando. *It means 'gradually slow down.' You usually see it at the end of a piece.*

accel—This is short for accelerando *and means "speed up."*

THE BLACK KEYS

The black keys open up a range of new sounds and moods on the piano. These keys are called **sharps** and **flats**. Sharps raise notes by half a tone and flats lower them. The signs that tell you to play them are called **accidentals**.

ACCIDENTALS ON THE PIANO KEYBOARD

There are three signs that are used when playing black keys.

STEP 1

This sign is called a sharp. When you see it before a note, it means play the next key to the right.

STEP 2

Practice finding sharps by playing these notes on the piano:

STEP 3

This sign is called a flat. When you see it before a note, it means play the next key to the left.

STEP 4

Try playing these flat notes on the piano:

STEP 5

This sign is the **natural**. When you see it, play the note without a sharp or a flat. If a note has been sharp, the natural sign resets it to normal.

Don't get fooled!

When you see a sharp or a flat sign in front of a note, play every matching note in that bar in the same way. But remember, when you get to the next bar it goes back to normal. Try not to get fooled when playing the exercise below.

MORE ADVANCED SKILLS

24

ELEPHANT PARADE

STEP 1

Put your knowledge into practice and have a stab at playing this piece of music. Your fingers start in the position shown right.

Musical direction

Look out for the accents and the speed change at the end. This gives the piece a bit of excitement. Turn back to page 23 to remember what these signs mean.

THE BLACK KEYS

ORIENTAL MIST

Trade secrets

This piece only uses black keys. Remember that all accidentals last for the whole bar unless canceled by a natural sign. Try holding down the right sustain pedal for the entire piece—it really adds to the effect.

STEP 1

Oriental Mist starts with your hands in this position. Remember to play legato.

STEP 2

Practice playing both hand parts separately before bringing them together. At bar 11, your hands should look like this (right).

26

ALLEYCATS

with a swing feel

Purr-fect rhythm

Practice the right hand rhythm carefully. Your left hand plays the same pattern of notes but moves to different positions on the keyboard.

STEP 1

Test your sight-reading by playing through the piece slowly. Start with your fingers in this position.

STEP 2

Concentrate on using a swing feel in both parts. This is how your hands look in bar 13.

27

SCALES

Scales are the core exercises of any skilled pianist. They allow you to gain fluidity and control in your playing. Learning scales can seem like hard work, but they are important to commanding the keyboard.

C MAJOR SCALE

STEP 1

The simplest scale to learn is C major. Remember to practice each hand separately first. Then slowly try to use them together.

There are several reasons why scales are important to practice:

- They are excellent warm-ups.
- They help you recognize, and play in, different keys.
- They allow you to become familiar with the keyboard.
- They help train your brain to remember patterns.
- A lot of pieces use scale patterns, so you will already know them when you need them.

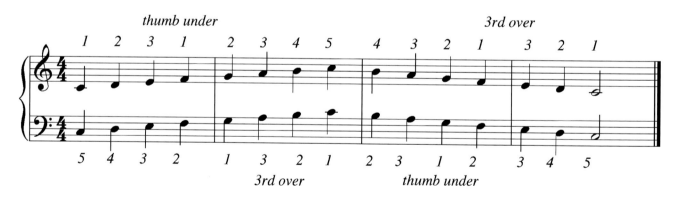

Tips for practicing scales:

- *Make sure to play them at the same speed.*
- *The notes need to be even—listen carefully when you are playing them.*
- *Make sure that your wrist stays relaxed and in the same position as it moves up and down the piano.*
- *Certain notes or patterns can help you. For instance, in C major, finger 3 on both hands land together, first on E and then on A.*

KEY SIGNATURES

Pieces of music can be in different keys. Each key has a different number of sharps or flats to make its characteristic sound. A **key signature**—which is written at the beginning of a piece—tells you which notes are sharp and flat.

THE KEY OF G MAJOR

Key signature for G major.
All the Fs are sharp.

 ### THE KEY OF F MAJOR

Key signature for F major.
All the Bs are flat.

Handy signatures

A key signature tells you that every time you play a particular note it is sharp or flat. You no longer have to read a sharp or flat every time you play the note. Learn which notes are sharpened or flattened in each key signature. You will improve a lot!

Tonics

The main note in the key is the first note in the scale. This is called the **tonic**.

G MAJOR SCALE
STEP 1

Place your fingers in the starting position shown. Remember all the F notes are sharp.

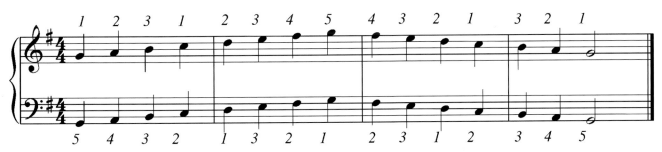

F MAJOR SCALE
STEP 1

F major starting position.
Remember all the B notes are flat.

MINOR SCALES

When you listen to pieces in a major key they sound happy. When you hear them in a minor key they sound sad. Here are some scale patterns for minor keys.

A MINOR SCALE

STEP 1

The A minor scale looks like this. Place your fingers in their starting positions and practice playing the scale evenly.

30

D MINOR SCALE

STEP 1

This is the scale of D minor. The starting positions for your fingers are shown on the right.

Relative minor and relative major keys

C major and A minor have the same key signature (no sharps or flats). For each major scale, there is a minor scale which has the same key signature—we describe them as related. Therefore, A minor is the "relative minor" of C major, and C major is the "relative major" of A minor.

MORE ADVANCED SKILLS

SCALE EXERCISES

Try these scale exercises to add variety to your scale practice.

EXERCISE 31.1

EXERCISE 31.2

CHORDS & ARPEGGIOS

When you play several notes together on the piano, you are playing a chord. These solid combinations can be broken up to create beautiful cascades of notes called arpeggios. Chords appear more often as you play more challenging pieces, so they are definitely worth mastering

HOW TO PLAY CHORDS

To play the main chord for any key signature, play the main note of the scale (the tonic) together with the third note and the fifth note. This is called a **triad**.

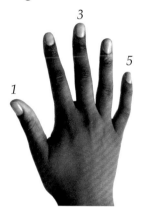

STEP 1

Put your right-hand thumb on middle C with a relaxed hand position. Then play your third and fifth finger at the same time—you have just played the chord of C major.

STEP 2

Try the following chords. Remember to check the key signatures first.

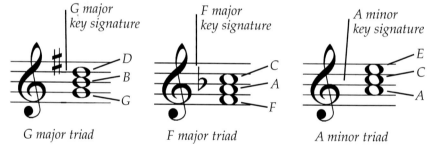

G major key signature
D
B
G
G major triad

F major key signature
C
A
F
F major triad

A minor key signature
E
C
A
A minor triad

HOW TO PLAY ARPEGGIOS

Arpeggios are when you play the notes that make up a chord separately, so that you can hear each note in turn in a particular pattern.

STEP 1

Place your hands on the keyboard with the fingering shown below. Then play one note after another, remembering to check the fingering. Practice hands separately first, then put them together.

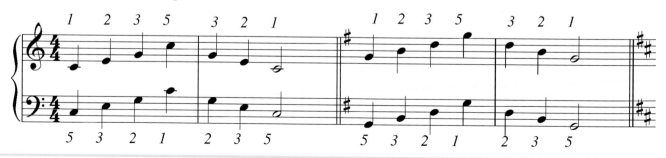

MORE ADVANCED SKILLS

STEP 2

This is a minor arpeggio, which means it uses these notes of the minor scale.

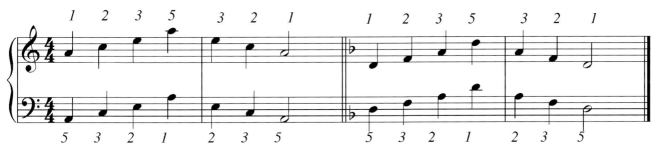

STEP 3

Once you feel ready, try this exercise, which uses eighth-notes.

HOW TO PLAY BROKEN CHORDS

Broken chords also play the notes that make up a chord, but in a different pattern to an arpeggio.

STEP 1

Try the following broken chord in C major. Once you have learned the fingering, play a D minor broken chord (thumb and 5th finger on D), an A minor broken chord (thumb and 5th on A) and an F major broken chord (thumb and 5th on F).

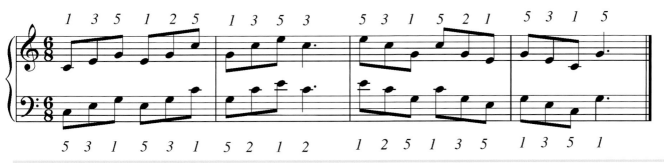

SIGHT-READING

Imagine putting a piece of music in front of yourself and being able to play it without having to slowly work out the notes, the hand positions, or the key and time signatures. All of this is possible, with a little work and practice.

HOW TO SIGHT-READ

You may not have realized it, but you have already built up your sight-reading skills by practicing the exercises in this book. Here are a few tips on what to look for when you see a piece for the first time.

STEP 1

Check the time signature.

STEP 2

Check the key signature. Then scan quickly through the piece to see if any notes are sharp or flat.

STEP 3

Spot any position changes before you start and work out how you are going to play them.

EXERCISE 34.1

STEP 4

Check the direction on tempo, and start your playing at a comfortable speed.

Sight-reader's guide:
- *Look for repeating patterns.*
- *Try to spot chords and arpeggios that you already know.*
- *Look for any change of dynamics.*

34

MORE SIGHT-READING EXERCISES

Practice your sight-reading with the exercises below:

EXERCISE 35.1

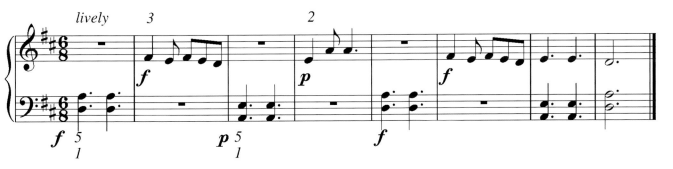

EXERCISE 35.2

EXERCISE 35.3

TRAIN YOUR EARS

Having a "good pair of ears" is an important part of being a musician. They will help you to keep a steady pulse, or beat, recognize wrong notes, improve your singing voice, and even enable you to play a piece of music just by listening to it.

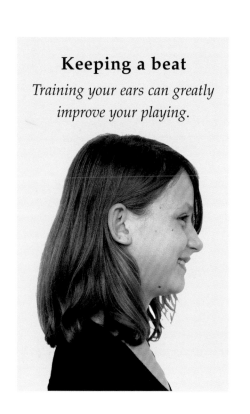

Keeping a beat
Training your ears can greatly improve your playing.

STEP 1

Tap along to the beat whenever you are listening to music. Make sure you stay steady. Try to work out how many beats are in each bar. Can you tell the time signature just by listening?

STEP 2

Test your ears—can you recognize notes and rhythms that sound "off"? The following phrases are taken from pieces in this book. See if you can figure out which notes or rhythms are wrong. You may need to play through the original once or twice first.

PHRASE FROM *SHAPES IN MOTION* (PAGE 21)

PHRASE FROM *ELEPHANT PARADE* (PAGE 25)

DEVELOPING YOUR SINGING

Singing is a great way to improve your musical ear.
It helps you to "hear" the notes in your head.

Play through the phrases below. Then sing or hum
them back to yourself. Check your singing by
playing the phrases back after you have sung them.

EXERCISE 37.1

EXERCISE 37.2

TRAINING BOOT CAMP

With practice, you will be able to figure out how to play tunes that you have heard.
Think of a song that you know, and see if you can work out how to play it on the piano.
The more you practice, the quicker and more accurate you will become at this skill.

PIANO PIECES

The pieces on the following pages use the techniques you have learned in this book. Remember to flip back to the basics pages if you are not sure about something.

LAZY DAYS

STEP 1

Place your hands on the keys as shown. This piece has a laid-back legato style (page 16). Concentrate on the left-hand slurs.

STEP 2

At bar 13, your fingers look like this.

TANGO EXPRESS

STEP 1

Start with your fingers in this position (right).
Practice both of your hands separately.
Pay close attention to your right hand.

STEP 2

Try it hands together, slowly, bar by bar, using
the Five Times Rule (**see** page 6). By bar 13, your
hands will be in this position (left).

STEP 3

Now add in all the colorful parts—the dynamics
and the staccato stab—to get that sassy tango feeling.

Stab that rhythm!

*The staccato notes in the left hand
make a rhythm typical of tango.*

SLIMY UNDERGROUND

This piece uses the otherworldly sound of the chromatic scale—
a scale made up of all the white keys and black notes next to each
other. Now place your fingers in the starting position (left) and play.

Acciaccaturas

The last two bars contain two "grace notes" called 'acciaccaturas' (say 'ak-chak-a-to-rah'). Play these notes immediately before the main note without any gap between.

SUNNY DAYS

STEP 1

This is a happy-sounding piece, so play it brightly.
Start with your hands as shown (right) and practice
both parts separately and slowly.

Key signature

*Don't forget
the F sharps
in this piece.*

STEP 2

In bar 11, your hands will be in this
position. Look out for the CODA at
the end.

41

THE SNAKE CHARMER

steady and with mystery

Accidentals will happen

Remember that accidentals are sharp or flat notes, most often played on the black keys.

STEP 1

Accidentals give this piece a mystical feel. Start with your fingers as shown (left).

STEP 2

Practice both hands separately, paying attention to the right hand. The finger position in bar nine is shown (right).

42

Bb BOOGIE
STEP 1

Boogie woogie and stride piano are modern musical forms that really rock. Start slowly with your fingers in this position. Remember—speed can come later.

Starting position

43

CLOCKWORK

STEP 1

Start slowly with your fingers in the position shown (right). Concentrate on getting the rhythm of the piece correct. The more you practice, the smoother your playing will become.

Right-hand shape

Keep your right hand in the same shape through most of this piece, by simply moving it from note to note.

STEP 2

Once you get both hands working together, everything will click. Your fingers should hit this position (right) in bar 11.

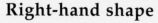

PAVEMENT CRACKS

STEP 1

Here's a piece for you to try. It will test your sight-reading and all the skills you have learned in this book.

Watch the hands!

This piece uses many hand positions.
Scan through the music and find them.
Then make sure you practice them first.

45

GREAT PIANO PLAYERS

All pianists play for their own enjoyment, as well as that of their family and friends. For some talented people, playing becomes a career. Sergei Rachmaninoff and Oscar Peterson were both famous and successful pianists and composers who played to huge audiences all over the world.

SERGEI RACHMANINOFF

Rachmaninoff was born in Russia, in 1873 and died in Beverley Hills, California, in 1943. As well as being a fantastic pianist, Sergei Rachmaninoff was a famous composer. Some of his most famous compositions are his Piano Concertos Nos. 2 and 3, as well as a piece called *Rhapsody on a Theme by Paganini* (1934). Rachmaninoff was a tall man, over 6 feet (1.8 meters) tall and had huge hands. It was said that Rachmaninoff could play a chord of C, Eb, G, C, and G with one hand! That's pretty amazing—and very useful if you are a pianist.

OSCAR PETERSON

Oscar Peterson was born in Canada in 1925 and died in Montreal, Quebec, in 2007. Oscar Emmanuel Peterson (or OP to his friends) was one of the finest jazz pianists and composers ever. He recorded his first single when he was 19 and went on to record 200 albums and win eight Grammy awards. He was known for his energetic and virtuosic performances. See if you can find a recording of him and have a listen.

How to progress with your playing

- *Get into a regular routine of practicing, using the tips in this book.*
- *Don't give up if you sometimes find it hard—keep trying!*
- *Find a good teacher who can guide your learning and give confidence.*
- *Always play some music that you really like to motivate you.*
- *Finally, always ENJOY IT!*

GLOSSARY

accel. Get faster, gradually

accent Stress the note

accidental An accidental changes the pitch of a note

adagio Slow tempo

allegro Fast tempo

allegretto Fairly fast tempo

andante Quite slow tempo

dynamics How loud or quiet the music should be played

flat Play the next key (usually black)to the left

key signatures How many sharps and/or flats in a piece

largo Very slow tempo

legato Smoothly

moderato Moderate tempo

natural Play the original note

presto Very fast tempo

repeat Repeat the section between the repeat signs

rit. Slow down, gradually

sharp Play the next key (usually black) to the right

staccato Detached notes, played punchily

tempo The pace of the music – how fast or slow it goes

time signature How many beats, and of what type, in a bar

tonic The main, and first, note of a scale or key signature

triad A three-note chord

vivace Lively and fast tempo

INDEX

48